IN THE
NATIONAL INTEREST

General Sir John Monash once exhorted a graduating class to 'equip yourself for life, not solely for your own benefit but for the benefit of the whole community'. At the university established in his name, we repeat this statement to our own graduating classes, to acknowledge how important it is that common or public good flows from education.

Universities spread and build on the knowledge they acquire through scholarship in many ways, well beyond the transmission of this learning through education. It is a necessary part of a university's role to debate its findings, not only with other researchers and scholars, but also with the broader community in which it resides.

Publishing for the benefit of society is an important part of a university's commitment to free intellectual inquiry. A university provides civil space for such inquiry by its scholars, as well as for investigations by public intellectuals and expert practitioners.

This series, In the National Interest, embodies Monash University's mission to extend knowledge and encourage informed debate about matters of great significance to Australia's future.

Professor Margaret Gardner AC
President and Vice-Chancellor,
Monash University

ABUL RIZVI

POPULATION SHOCK

MONASH
UNIVERSITY
PUBLISHING

Monash University Publishing
Matheson Library Annexe
40 Exhibition Walk
Monash University
Clayton, Victoria 3800, Australia
https://publishing.monash.edu

Monash University Publishing brings to the world publications which advance the best traditions of humane and enlightened thought.

ISBN: 9781922464828 (paperback)
ISBN: 9781922464835 (ebook)

Series: In the National Interest
Editor: Louise Adler
Project manager & copyeditor: Paul Smitz
Designer: Peter Long
Typesetter: Cannon Typesetting
Proofreader: Gillian Armitage
Printed in Australia by Ligare Book Printers

A catalogue record for this book is available from the National Library of Australia.

The paper this book is printed on is in accordance with the standards of the Forest Stewardship Council®. The FSC® promotes environmentally responsible, socially beneficial and economically viable management of the world's forests.

POPULATION SHOCK

The year 2001 was a hugely significant one for Australia. Ask most politically minded people and they'll name one of two major events that shaped the future of our nation: the September 11 terrorist attacks on the World Trade Center buildings in New York, and the Howard government's refusal to let the Norwegian freighter *MV Tampa*, carrying 433 rescued asylum seekers, enter Australian waters. The first is a day etched in minds across the globe, the beginning of a new period of uncertainty and fear. The second divided Australian voters into two camps: those who desired harsher borders, and those who wanted to take a more compassionate approach to people hoping for refuge. The asylum-seeker debate would dominate the next federal election and shape political discussions for many years.

But neither of these events had as great an impact on Australia as a series of mostly unnoticed regulatory changes to immigration policy that were made in the same year. Those changes have seen Australia become the youngest, most diverse and fastest-growing nation in the developed world. They made our economy stronger than it otherwise would have been. They helped businesses to thrive and families to grow. They rapidly expanded our international education industry into our third-biggest export earner and revitalised the CBDs of our major cities. The changes meant more young people were welcomed from overseas, initially as students and working holiday-makers. But many of those young people would go on to become the partners, husbands and wives of Australians, as well as the fathers and mothers of future Australians.

A QUIET REVOLUTION

Contrary to the public narrative, the Howard government's immigration minister, Philip Ruddock, didn't want to cut the migration program when his party came to power in 1996. There was no mention of slashing immigration numbers in the Coalition's election platform. In fact, Ruddock happily signed off on a now publicly available Cabinet submission to expand the size of the program. But Howard wouldn't have it.

Along with Helen Williams, who was the new secretary of the Department of Immigration, I was the public servant called into the prime minister's office in the opening months of what for him would become twelve years in the job, and asked to explain where immigration could be cut. The prime minister didn't ask questions about why my colleagues and I were advising the government to expand immigration. He'd made his decision. Howard wanted to know which permanent visa categories he could cut and by how much. He was not happy when I said there were legal limits to the cuts he could make without amending the legislation. That triggered a series of changes to the *Migration Act 1958* and associated regulations that parliament would debate for the next eighteen months—the Senate would pass some of the changes but reject many others. (Do not be mistaken here: my first encounter with John Howard took place many months before an infamous red-headed woman from Queensland made her maiden speech to parliament.)

And so the program was cut significantly in 1996–97 and again in 1997–98. Family migration was restricted, including a cap on the number of Australians who could sponsor their parents to come here. The skilled migration program was tightened. Most skilled migrants had to meet a new minimum English-language test and could be no older than forty-five. Their skills had to be assessed as meeting Australian standards by the relevant independent body appointed by the minister. The Howard government also reduced our humanitarian intake.

Howard was convinced that immigration increased unemployment. Instead of viewing migrants in terms of the potential benefits they brought to Australia, including filling key jobs, increasing business investment, buying our goods and services, renting locally owned homes and paying taxes—as he had earlier in his political career—he now saw them as a burden. Howard was not interested in the research evidence. Skilled migrants who arrive near the start of their careers and fill key skills gaps immediately begin contributing to both the supply side of the economy (what they produce) and the demand side of the economy (the spending they do to set up and run a new household). The reality is that they create more jobs than they take. Because of their age and skill profile, they help increase productivity and thereby wages growth—unless government policy is to actively suppress wages growth. The costs of their education have been borne by another country while the benefits largely accrue to the receiving country, offset marginally by any money they send back home. And because of their age, they slow the rate of ageing.

Howard's cuts to the migration program now form part of the popular folklore. But at the time, they came out of nowhere for journalists, parliamentarians and certainly us in the public service. For the next three years, the anti-immigration agenda became a calling card of the Howard government. Pauline Hanson, who entered parliament whipping up anti-Asian sentiment in the community, was never publicly chastised by the prime minister. It took years for Howard to be convinced to introduce an anti-racism strategy and to publicly utter the word 'multiculturalism'.

Xenophobia aside, the public service was concerned. We could see that the 1990s would have the lowest rate of net migration of any decade since World War II. Combined with the steady decline in fertility since the 1990–91 recession, Australia was facing a worrying new phenomenon. Our projections showed the population beginning to age more rapidly. So, as a diligent public servant, I convinced minister Ruddock to commission research on our long-term population future. Professor Peter McDonald of the Australian National University, now the pre-eminent voice on population policy in this country, and his colleague Dr Rebecca Kippen did the research for us, which was published in 1999.[1]

What the researchers told us was even worse than I'd suspected. Their paper included a series of so-called population pyramid projections. Now, many high school and first-year university students are introduced to the population pyramid. It's a triangular graph showing that more of a nation's people are in younger age groups and smaller numbers are in older age groups. McDonald and Kippen showed Australia's traditional population pyramid gradually changing shape from a triangle to something more resembling a coffin, with a large cohort of elderly baby boomers forming the top of it. Instead of lots of younger people and fewer older people, Australia was headed towards fewer younger people and a bulge of people beyond working age.

I was nervous about briefing minister Ruddock on the paper. His public persona was not that of a friendly, cuddly sort of guy at the best of times. Thankfully, Ruddock had a thorough understanding of immigration policy. Regardless of whether you liked his politics, he'd been immersing himself in the area for years before he got the job of immigration minister. He also had impeccable attention to detail. He understood the implications of the coffin-shaped graphs immediately.

The implications of population ageing had not gone unnoticed by other government departments and agencies. Treasury and the Productivity Commission were concerned. The Australian Bureau of

Statistics' population projections for 1999 showed Australia's median age rising to forty-one by 2021 and to forty-six by 2051. One of Australia's most prominent economists, Glenn Withers, wrote an influential paper on population ageing in Australia.[2] The business community were beginning to talk about ageing too, and the editors of major Australian newspapers were also paying attention. Apart from NSW premier Bob Carr—a longstanding opponent of immigration—it also worried state governments. It was enough for treasurer Peter Costello and Ruddock to convince John Howard, albeit reluctantly, to gradually start increasing immigration.

Ruddock insisted the increase had to be delivered without compromising on the skill level of migrants. However, the skill-selection criteria the government had previously tightened had delivered both an improvement in labour force outcomes as well as an inevitable decline in applications. Potential migrants who couldn't meet the new criteria responded by taking their interest elsewhere. Australia was simply not generating enough applications, which meant there was no excess from which to draw. So how could we grow the migration program? Given Ruddock's condition, which was a fair one in my view, there was only one workable approach: Australia would increase the numbers of both overseas students and working holiday-makers. Once they'd arrived in the country and sufficiently upskilled, they'd be allowed to apply for permanent residency. Critically, they could do this without having to go back home.

It was no quick fix. If it was to work, it would do so slowly and attract ongoing criticism from business for failing to be sufficiently responsive. On the other hand, there was a risk that it would work too well and application numbers would get out of control. There was also the risk that some students and working holiday-makers would fall into a kind of immigration limbo—unable or unwilling to go home and unable to access permanent residence. They could also be subject to employer exploitation. All risks had to be managed.

The approach of growing temporary migration with explicit pathways to permanent residence was anathema to longstanding officials in the Immigration Department. It overturned forty years of traditional immigration policy. Previously, the expectation had always been that overseas entrants applied for the visa they wanted while still outside of Australia. The shift was contrary to established wisdom and continues to be viewed today by many as 'backdoor migration'. It's not.

Preparing for such massive changes took us eighteen months: getting the regulations drafted, developing public information, changing information technology systems, and training staff not just in Australia but also at our overseas posts to deliver the new arrangements. The new system was implemented on 1 July 2001. In doing so, we were looking to entirely overhaul the size and shape of Australia's migration system. Bringing in younger people, encouraging them to acquire the skills they needed to succeed, and deliberately welcoming them to become part of a new country: it was novel. If it worked, we expected it would significantly slow the rate of population ageing and push back the day that deaths would start exceeding births in Australia.

The Immigration Department changed the way Australia processed overseas student and working holiday-maker visa applications. We changed Australia's famed points test to give successful overseas students a clear advantage, particularly if they studied outside the major cities of Sydney and Melbourne. It is to minister Ruddock's eternal credit that he strongly supported the changes and explained them to the public at his regular community consultations. The changes were seemingly so small, however, that the media barely noticed. They were preoccupied with sexier headline-grabbing topics. But those 1 July 2001 amendments to the migration regulations changed Australia forever.

Over the twenty years since, around two million overseas students and working holiday-makers have come to this country and been counted as part of net migration and thus the Australian population. A large number have gone on to become permanent residents and citizens.

THE 2002 *INTERGENERATIONAL REPORT*

In Australia's first *Intergenerational Report*, published in 2002, treasurer Peter Costello formalised what we'd set in motion. These reports, typically produced every five years, lay out Australia's plan for its future society, economy and population, projecting up to forty years ahead. The 2002 *Intergenerational Report* said that if Australia kept ageing at the then rate, from the decade of the 2020s the consequences would be severe. Economic growth would slow significantly, per-capita tax revenue would fall, and the cost of looking after older Australians would rapidly increase government debt. Presenting the report as he did was a deliberate decision by the treasurer: Costello wanted to scare people into changing their thinking, to help them understand what an enormous challenge lay ahead. Without significant intervention on population, Australia—the once lucky country—was headed for a bleak future.

Among the policy announcements made around this time was the much-discussed baby bonus. In selling this cash gift for new parents to the electorate, Costello infamously asked Australian women to have 'one for yourself, one for your husband and one for the country'. This too was designed to slow the rate of ageing and its negative impact on the Australian economy.

In 2002, Costello forecast only a modest rate of increase in net migration. This was because at the time we had no idea how much additional interest in studying and migrating to Australia the July 2001 changes would actually generate. We were trying something that hadn't been done before and we couldn't be certain it would work. I watched those numbers like a hawk, wondering how our experiment might land.

So, did the overall change in policy direction from July 2001 work out for Australia? The answer, at least to a certain extent, is yes. Net migration to Australia ever since has been significantly higher than was forecast in the 2002 *Intergenerational Report*, and the international education industry has grown much faster than we ever imagined—albeit it is possible for the industry to grow too fast, which at times it has. Australia's population is the youngest in the developed world. We have a higher proportion of our population born overseas than any other developed nation. And prior to shutting our borders in the wake of COVID-19, we were also the fastest-growing population in the developed world. We have slowed the impact of ageing in an extraordinarily effective way. Australia is the envy of its global counterparts. Even international leaders, such as UK Prime Minister Boris Johnson, have talked about the Australian model of immigration with envy.

But you cannot outrun ageing and death forever.

THE 100-YEAR POPULATION SHOCK

Baby boomers have a tendency to think of themselves as special. And they have indeed shaped government policy unlike any other demographic. This is the case not only in Australia but across most of the world. The post-war baby boom of the late 1940s and 1950s created a population shock that will continue to evolve over the course of this enormous generation's life, roughly a century from when the first boomers were born in the late 1940s through to when the last boomers are likely to die in the 2050s. While long-term population directions, in terms of both size and age composition, have always driven the destiny of nations, the baby boomers are different. They followed a comparably small generation whose lives were defined by the low birth rates of the Great Depression and the higher death rates caused by World War II. And they preceded generation X and the millennials, whose parents had far greater access to a handy little tool called contraception and much higher levels of schooling, particularly the education of girls and young women.

The boomers formed an enormous bubble that has slowly made its way through the traditional population pyramid from bottom to top. This has resulted in what will ultimately be a 100-year-long population shock to economies and societies across the world, as the boomers continue through the human life cycle.

Most of us have grown up with warnings about overpopulation. In 1968, Paul and Anne Ehrlich predicted worldwide famine and environmental degradation because of it. Their phenomenally popular book *The Population Bomb* turbocharged global fear of overpopulation and set up 'zero population growth' movements around the world.[3] China's one-child policy, formally implemented in 1980, was a response to that fear, with appalling consequences that continue to reverberate today due to the imbalance between males and females in that enormous country (albeit China acknowledged this was a serious issue by permitting families to have two children from 2015, upping the number to three in May 2021). These policies and theories were misguided. While the period from 1950 to 2020 saw extraordinary population growth because of the baby boomers and their children, what will eventually follow is a period of severe population ageing and then decline.

What was never anticipated by Paul and Anne Ehrlich, and indeed the famous Thomas Malthus who wrote about these issues in the 1700s, was the transition to low fertility rates. The pill, a revolutionary advancement that allowed women to control their own reproduction, at the same time increasing their education prospects and empowerment, meant that fertility in the developed world would fall below two births per woman, starting in the 1970s and continuing today. This meant that the world was not at risk of overpopulation in the way it might have been. In fact, the combination of baby boomers' ageing and a decrease in births worldwide will eventually lead to the global population peaking, most likely in the second half of this century, and then steadily declining. While some environmentalists might welcome a decreasing population, even the environmental benefits are limited if we are unable to afford the policies needed to address climate change. Economies, societies and governments will actually experience a severe shock as the death of the baby boomers prompts population decline in much of the developed world, and eventually all of the world.

The 2021 *Intergenerational Report*, released in June, covers the next forty years, when Australia will age significantly more. To better understand the context for the 2021 report, there is merit in considering the population shock that the transition to low fertility has created, a shock comprising four broad stages.

STAGE ONE: THE BOOMERS IN CHILDHOOD

In Australia, the impact of the baby boomers was magnified by large waves of post–World War II migration. My own family migrated here in early 1966 as part of the first cohort of non-European arrivals when then prime minister Harold Holt began dismantling the White Australia policy. I was seven years old when we left everything familiar behind in India. There were no brown or black faces at my suburban Canberra school, certainly no other kids with peculiar Muslim names. I was a curiosity to both my teachers and schoolmates. The modest way my mother dressed, my father's daily prayers, the food we ate at home: all were completely foreign to my new friends. And I had a lot of friends. Not because I was especially popular, but because my class was enormous. There were more than forty students crammed into rooms built for twenty-five. My primary school seemed to be adding a new portable classroom every year to accommodate demand. In the middle of a Canberra winter, these were really, really cold—until the heater got going, then we'd all be peeling off layers of clothes because it was so hot in those metal boxes.

Australia's population growth averaged a phenomenal 2.4 per cent per annum during the 1950s and almost 2 per cent per annum during the 1960s. But while we were certainly a leader in population growth, we were not alone. Other migrant settler nations were also growing rapidly, making the most of the opportunities brought by population expansion to invest in new infrastructure, develop new industries and grow their economies. The baby boom and post-war migration and reconstruction enabled many developed nations to repay the enormous government debts they had accumulated during World War II. Critically, while populations were growing rapidly, *working age* populations were not growing as fast. The large number of babies and children meant that the ratio of working age people to the population as a whole either declined or remained relatively low. In many nations, the percentage of the population who were of working age was substantially below 60 per cent, and often near 50 per cent. This working-age-to-population (WAP) ratio is a key marker of ageing that I will continue to refer to in this book. (My millennial daughters wish me to assure the reader that this is very different to popstar Cardi B's version.)

The 1950s and 1960s were also a highly egalitarian period in most developed nations. The wealth of the top 10 per cent of the population was comparatively low.[4] Highly progressive taxation rates ensured a more equal distribution of this wealth. Indeed, it was not unusual for developed nations to have a top marginal tax rate well above 70 per cent, and most nations had a substantial inheritance tax. In Australia, the states did not completely abolish death duties until 1979.

The wage share of the economy compared with the capital income share during the 1950s and 1960s was also much higher than we see today across most of the developed world.[5] The average person going to work and earning a wage made up a comparatively greater share of gross domestic product than the incomes of companies and asset owners. This is quite unlike the situation today, where people who own multiple houses, company shares and indeed the companies themselves, have a greater portion of income and wealth than workers who only have their own labour to sell. Real wages grew strongly during the first stage of the population shock because workers were powerful, which correlated with high levels of union membership. In many developed nations, including Australia, union membership during the

1950s amounted to more than half the working population—if a union decided to strike, this could cripple an employer, even an entire industry.

The salaries of the chief executive officers of major corporations in the 1950s and 1960s were rarely more than twenty-five times those of base-level workers in the same corporation. That may sound like a big number, but today it's not unusual to see CEO salaries at well over 100 times those of entry-level personnel. In some instances, the person at the top of a company ladder earns close to 200 times more than the people on the bottom rung. In the 1970s, management guru Peter Drucker argued that ratios like this would risk damaging staff morale and worker productivity. It's a proposition that's awfully difficult to refute, although some governments have found ways to blame other segments of society for this situation.

As a migrant boy from India, growing up in suburban Canberra, I experienced neither great wealth nor great poverty. Each suburb in the Australian capital had both larger, privately built houses and smaller, government-built homes and flats. Almost all the kids went to a local government or Catholic school. We played for local sports teams rather than going to wealthy private schools that ran their own. It's almost a cliché to idealise a bygone era, but the fact is, times were simpler. Work was plentiful for those who wanted it. Workers could earn a good, liveable wage that wasn't all that different to that of the family next door. Despite rapid population growth, most young workers could afford to buy a house, and home ownership increased rapidly. During stage one of the population shock, Australian society was fairer and more egalitarian.

STAGE TWO: THE BOOMERS
IN ADULTHOOD

My wife came home from work one afternoon in 1982 and told me she'd been sacked. I wasn't surprised. Helen had been a relief teacher for a short period after she'd graduated from university. She'd only recently cleared her probation as a permanent teacher when the union strikes got serious. Teachers were campaigning for better pay and better conditions, including time out of the classroom each week for lesson planning. At that time, pretty much every teacher was in the union, and if you weren't, you were ostracised. Such was the strength of the education union.

At the peak of the campaign, Helen and her colleagues were striking weekly for half a school day, creating havoc in the education system. During those strikes, the teachers would gather at the basketball arena at the Australian Institute of Sport because there were simply too many of them to fit in a regular hall. They'd lose half a day's pay, but I recall that Helen used to quite enjoy those meetings. It was a chance to catch up with old friends from teachers' college, in-between the more serious business of speeches and votes.

One day the government threats reached boiling point and the Canberra public school teaching workforce was sacked en masse. But the ultimatum couldn't be maintained. The schools didn't function without teachers, and parents couldn't go to work. The morning after being fired, Helen and her colleagues met at a bowling club and shared a few drinks. By lunchtime they'd been reinstated. They walked back to school to begin their classes again, and the union won its fight.

By the late 1960s or early 1970s, most developed nations had reached the second stage of the population shock. The baby boomers were now grown up and entering the labour market in huge numbers. This caused the all-important WAP ratio to begin rising, creating the 'demographic dividend' phase in each nation's history; that is, the period in which nations could be most rewarded for the enormous baby boomer population bubble.

In Australia, the surge of boomers setting up new households and entering the workforce, including women and girls in numbers like never before, created major policy challenges as well as opportunities.

Most young families are spenders not savers. They buy houses for their growing families to live in and cars to transport them around. They take holidays for four or five people, not two, and purchase trolleys full of groceries. The spending of these young adult boomers was further assisted by tax rates that were much more progressive than those of today. This, combined with strong unions that frequently used their industrial muscle to secure large wage increases, furiously stoked growth in private consumption, which in turn drove up inflation and meant the powerful unions continued to demand even further wage increases.

Women, now able to control when they had babies for the first time in history, were able to plan for their careers. They started to have fewer babies, often not having their first until well into their twenties—down the track, the baby boomers' children would generally prefer not to have their first baby until they turned thirty, or even later. Baby boomer women entered the workforce in greater numbers, exacerbating the already rapid expansion of the labour force. Two-income households became more common, allowing for even faster growth in private consumption.

As tail-end baby boomers, my wife and I both started full-time work in the early 1980s. That enabled us to buy our first home relatively young by today's standards and to later have our two daughters.

We went from happily impoverished university students to thriving employees who could afford to set up a home and grow our family, thanks to salaries that were increasing well ahead of inflation. In this, we were typical of our generation.

As the baby boomers set new spending records, developed nations began implementing tighter fiscal and monetary policies in response to rising inflation. With limits on capital availability, government spending was leaving businesses with few opportunities to borrow money other than at rising interest rates. Governments were crowding out the private sector's access to the very capital they needed to grow. This, in tandem with the oil shock of the 1970s, caused much of the developed world to experience the unusual phenomenon of stagflation: simultaneously high inflation and unemployment.

The supply-side economic policies of Western leaders such as Ronald Reagan in the United States, Margaret Thatcher in the United Kingdom and Malcolm Fraser in Australia were designed to cope with the consequences of rapid workforce growth, surging demand and runaway inflation. They prioritised fighting inflation first by limiting the supply of money in the economy and increasing interest rates. They implemented industrial relations reforms to rein in wage growth, enabling more flexible hiring and firing and curbing union power. They cut company tax rates so that businesses had more funds available to expand their productive capacity to cater for rapidly rising private consumption expenditure.

And, of course, they privatised traditionally government functions. As they gradually ran out of things to privatise, they started targeting utility services such as water, electricity and telecommunications—all with the intention of rapidly creating new opportunities for business. The artificially manufactured markets for traditional utility functions often led to single, large, private companies delivering essential services in their designated area. The consequences of this mass sale of government-owned enterprises were often disastrous for ordinary people. For instance, the Howard government's sale of Telstra had long-term and wide-reaching impacts: it ultimately caused Australia to be a laggard in the development of broadband, the crucial infrastructure of the twenty-first century.

Shrinking the role of government as much as possible was viewed by Reagan, Thatcher and Fraser as the ideal means of increasing economic growth. It certainly increased the wealth of the uber-rich, who led the self-interested charge for increased privatisation and turbocharged the rise in inequality.

From the 1980s, government policies also created 'incentives' for aspirational families to work harder.

Many developed nations reduced marginal tax rates for high-income earners while also reducing the tax on capital income. This way, people who earned their living from capital, rather than from wages, were better rewarded. The idea was to encourage lower-income workers to work harder and aspire to the status of the rich holders of capital. A suite of policies was adopted in this vein. Some countries flattened their income tax structures; others implemented new consumption taxes that were regressive and hit poorer people harder; some countries did both. In Australia, most state governments abolished inheritance taxes. The Thatcher government's 'poll tax' was an extreme manifestation of that thinking—for the privilege of being an adult who lived in Britain, every adult citizen was charged a flat-rate tax just for existing. Thatcher was soon thrown out of office and her successor abandoned the poll tax.

The second stage of the population shock also triggered a steady decline in union membership and the ability of unions to secure wage increases. The union movement was incredibly strong in the 1970s and 1980s—and not just in the teaching profession. Every evening on the news, we'd hear that there were one or more unions either taking or threatening strike action. There was even a 1973 top-forty song by British band The Strawbs that celebrated union power as the means of always winning any wage demand. Union strength had grown globally in the first half of the twentieth century partly because unions were able to secure wage increases exclusively for their members. But the constant, disruptive striking behaviour eventually wore down the general public, who relied on teachers, construction workers, the shipping industry, bus drivers and nurses. This shift in public sentiment over time helped many governments to implement policies that steadily reduced union power—and with it the power of workers to win wage increases.

The approach of the Hawke government, elected in Australia in 1983, stood in stark contrast to the anti-union Thatcher, Reagan and Fraser governments. Hawke was a creature of the union movement, having previously been secretary of the Australian Council of Trade Unions, and the new prime minister sought to address existing economic challenges through greater cooperation between business and unions. This meant the reduction of Australia's near-constant industrial action was gradual and managed because of Hawke's Prices and Incomes Accord. Australia did not experience the abrupt and painful war with unions that the Thatcher government initiated, culminating in the United Kingdom's 'winter of discontent' in 1978–79. Australia did, however, ultimately adopt most of the supply-side policies of the era, including reducing the power of unions. Use of industrial action to secure wage increases became increasingly rare as the second stage of the population shock progressed into the 1990s and beyond.

The baby boomers' period of working adulthood continued their startling impact on economies and societies worldwide. The supply-side policies that were adopted in response to the second stage of the population shock sparked a fifty-year-long trend in the share of GDP earned by working people falling and the share going to owners of capital growing. The Reserve Bank of Australia has found the proportion of GDP that is made up of wages and salaries has steadily fallen since the 1970s. In Australia, the labour share of GDP fell from 65 per cent in 1980 to 52 per cent in 2018.[6] During that same period, the share of GDP represented by the operating surplus of companies increased from around 24 per cent to well over 35 per cent.

These outcomes are consistent with the economic hypothesis of Milton Friedman that many conservative governments have been enamoured of. Friedman, however, predicted that the 'benefits of ever rising company profits would eventually flow down to the general public due to the assumption of perfect competition'.[7] What we now call 'trickle-down economics' of course rarely held true, but the rate at which developed economies grew during the second stage of the population shock disguised much of the rise in inequality. The now famous memes of former banker turned former prime minister Malcolm Turnbull reaching down to give a homeless man a $5 note might not have been created until the 2010s, but the inequality that has led to the record numbers of homeless Australians we have today was created much earlier.

More-rapid technological change also contributed to the stagnating wages of lower-skilled workers, particularly older workers in traditional manufacturing jobs. Governments failed to invest in the reskilling of these workers, while businesses increasingly viewed training an old dog to do new tricks as 'not their job'. For some reason, business loves to call for much smaller governments whilst at the same time demanding government spend more money on assisting business, such as by delivering more training and retraining, or at least paying for private training providers. Paying business to increase investment has become core government policy.

From the late 1950s, international trade also rapidly expanded, further boosting aggregate demand as new markets developed. This accelerated growth in major developed economies, as well as emerging economies such as South Korea, Singapore, Malaysia,

Taiwan and, of course, China. In these nations, international trade brought millions of people out of poverty, but in some instances at the expense of low-skilled workers in developed economies. Prior to 2000, median US wages were around thirty-five times those of workers in China. Today, that multiple is less than five.[8]

By 2010, as more and more boomers started heading into retirement, the developed world's demographic dividend was well and truly over.

STAGE THREE: THE BOOMERS ARE AGEING

If you'd told me at twenty-one that I'd one day spend my leisure time playing golf and visiting tired old townships, I'd have laughed at you. But as you age, the activities that keep you entertained change. Along with much of the baby boomer generation, my wife and I have now retired from the workforce. Our daughters are adults, with partners, homes, cars and children of their own. Not yet elderly, we're in the bright and easy period of life where we have more free time than we've enjoyed since childhood. We're privileged to be able to fill that time joyfully. There are holidays spent with friends, overlapping with holidays spent visiting our children. We have the space to read more novels, listen to more music, go to concerts, see plays, host dinner parties, and write confronting books about the challenges of an ageing and declining population.

In your sixties and seventies, a lot of time is also spent visiting small country towns. Why, I am not quite sure. Recently my wife and I were walking through the main street of one such town in regional New South Wales. There is no need to name the place, as it is much like any other ageing country town anywhere in the developed world. Australian regional towns are not yet at the stage of those in Italy and Spain, where houses are being sold to people around the globe for 1 euro, as long as the purchaser commits to refurbishing the house. But there are the usual dusty antique shops, cafes that sell flat whites in a mug, and rusting monuments in a park listing the names of local young men lost to world wars. Some shopfronts are closed or closing down—many stand vacant, forgotten, with no prospect of another tenant. Children are few and far between. Younger people are generally sparse, having moved to the cities in search of work, financial security and a more cosmopolitan social life. There are usually only a few thriving businesses left: a grocery shop, a local health service desperately trying to recruit a doctor or nurse, an aged-care home and a funeral parlour. This beautiful old town was well and truly entering its twilight years.

We've all visited a place like the one I've described, both in Australia and elsewhere. Now imagine those towns as *nations*.

From around 2010, the developed world, including China and Russia, collectively entered the third stage of the 100-year population shock; that is, a falling WAP ratio. It's important to understand that this third stage started in different nations at different times. For example, much of Europe and Japan was impacted from the late 1980s and early 1990s, much earlier than nations like the United Kingdom, the United States and Australia. This was largely because of the comparative size of the baby boom in different countries, the larger immigration intakes in some countries, and the speed with which fertility rates declined. Across the developed world, the WAP ratio is now in steady decline as more baby boomers join the ranks of the retired and there are comparatively fewer young people able to work. The size of the population segments aged sixty-five and over, and indeed eighty-five and over, continue to rise strongly.

GDP growth is slowing. Wages have stagnated, despite unemployment rates that are comparatively lower than during the second stage of the population shock. Productivity growth is anaemic, household consumption is weak, and businesses are reluctant to invest without significant encouragement from government. In Australia, younger people can barely afford to get into the housing market, partly because of negative gearing and related policies. Although the recent reductions in interest rates appear to have changed that, at least in the short term, the experience of the Japanese housing market is one of ongoing weakness—population ageing and decline will eventually put downward pressure on house prices, even in Australia, although many people will still have very large mortgages.

Researchers have long highlighted the negative impact of population ageing, and the ramifications for national economies and government budgets. The slower economic growth that significantly aged nations are experiencing has not appeared suddenly. Population trends move slowly. Ageing in developed economies has been forecast since the mid-1980s. Some of the world's most prominent economists have been discussing the population-based causes of slow economic growth since the developed world collectively entered the third stage of the population shock, using the descriptor 'secular stagnation'. As in the case of dangerous climate change, the world's experts saw this coming. We cannot say we weren't warned.

Alvin Hansen, writing way back in 1938, described secular stagnation as 'sick recoveries which die in their infancy and depressions which feed on themselves and leave a hard and seemingly immovable core of unemployment'. Hansen noted that 'the combined effect of the decline in population growth ... weighs very heavily as an explanation for the failure of the recent recovery to reach full employment'.[9] In 1938, Nobel prize–winning economist Gunnar Myrdal argued that 'age distribution has consequences both for the productivity of people and for total consumptive demand'.[10] Fast-forward seventy-five years and another Nobel prize winner, Paul Krugman, placed demographic ageing at the centre of the secular stagnation hypothesis. He wrote that rapid growth in the labour force during the second half of the twentieth century 'made sustaining investment fairly easy: the business of providing Americans with new houses, new offices, and so on easily absorbed a fairly high fraction of GDP'.[11] Also in 2013, former US Treasury secretary Larry Summers said in a speech to the International Monetary Fund that 'the growth in the work force in the industrial world, is trailing off very, very substantially'.[12]

Modern research on population ageing points to it having a negative impact on both the supply and demand sides of the economy. On the supply side, ageing puts downward pressure on labour force participation in three ways. First, with a reduced number of working-age people compared with retired people, the portion of the adult population that is working starts to shrink. Second, as the portion of elderly people in a society increases, the productivity of the economy also declines. This is because adults are most productive in their forties—the decade in which they are both relatively recently educated and experienced, as well as less likely to be juggling the demands of small children. Third, ageing leads to weaker wages growth, which in turn impacts fertility. When young couples can't get a pay rise or find a better-paying job, they're less likely to want to expand their families. Having more children becomes part of a financial equation that doesn't add up.

On the demand side, ageing reduces per-capita private household consumption—a factor that has been much underestimated in the research. Put crudely, old people buy less stuff. While young families are purchasing the major assets and goods required to live the rest of their lives, retirees have already done this. The truism of the old couple hobbling down to the corner shop hand in hand to buy their weekly treat of a vanilla slice and a cappuccino, still holds for the vast majority of the elderly. Reduced private consumption slows business investment and that further reduces productivity and wage growth, creating a vicious cycle of gloomy economic and financial news. Regrettably, these are exactly the phenomena we have seen play out across the developed world in stage three of the population shock.

There is no practical level of immigration that can stop ageing. Very low fertility rates make population decline inevitable. However, immigration has helped slow the rate of ageing in the United States, the United Kingdom, Canada, New Zealand and Australia.[13] In contrast to other developed nations, plus China and Russia, the populations of these five countries are projected to continue to grow well into the second half of this century. Immigration has also changed the ethnic composition of these nations. Australia is now home to an overseas-born population of almost 30 per cent of our inhabitants, the highest of any major developed nation. Due to the post-war migration program, gradual abolition of the White Australia policy from 1966, and the major changes to immigration policy since July 2001, Australia has become the most multicultural nation on the planet. That has presented challenges, but it has brought with it far more in the way of opportunities. These include the critical chance to age more gradually than most other developed nations, and thereby be able to plan for and make the required adjustments with much less pain.

All developed nations are now deep in stage three of the population shock. During this stage, no major developed economy has been able to sustain the long-term levels of economic growth or per-capita economic growth they enjoyed during stage two; that is, once the WAP ratio has been in decline.

With the encouragement of the IMF, some nations attempted to achieve growth through budget austerity from about 2010. In Australia, the Abbott government endeavoured to execute this strategy as well. The 2014 Budget will go down in history as an absolute shocker. (This is a technical term.) It made significant changes to welfare, stripping back benefits to the lowest-income Australians. The prime minister's promise of 'no cuts to education, no cuts to health, no change to pensions and no cuts to the ABC or SBS' was well and truly broken. On all counts. Abbott also attempted to introduce a co-payment for Medicare, defer unemployment benefits for six months for young people, remove bulk billing, and raise the eligibility age for the age pension. While those changes didn't pass the Senate, the Abbott government did create enormous uncertainty in the economy, including in terms of energy and environmental policies. The IMF has since abandoned its growth-through-austerity idea, which is welcome news. And COVID-19 has ensured all nations are now using massive levels of deficit financing to prop up their economies, although conservative governments around the world will still want to make government expenditure as low as possible, even with significantly aged populations, rather than think about fixing the tax system.

Zero and even negative interest rates have been commonplace in stage three, with most nations' central banks forecasting little chance of these returning to more 'normal' levels. The experience during the 1930s suggests that low interest rates and population ageing are co-travellers—once again, predominantly due to weak private consumption expenditure. It makes sense that Australia's interest rates were relatively high for most of the second stage of the population shock, when the WAP ratio was steadily rising. When my wife and I bought our first home in the early 1980s, mortgage interest rates of well over 10 per cent were standard, and we lived through the 17 per cent mortgage interest rates of the early 1990s. My eldest daughter, by contrast, bought her first home when interest rates were around 5 per cent. One day, my five-year-old grandson might consider that prohibitive. Regardless of this pie-in-the-sky prediction, Australians are unlikely to see mortgage interest rates in double figures ever again.

Gross government debt in most developed nations is now approaching 100 per cent of GDP; Japan's is over 200 per cent and rising rapidly. Even pre-COVID-19, budget deficits had become endemic in particularly aged societies, as ageing populations drive down per-capita tax revenue and raise health, aged-care and pension costs. The COVID-19 recession will only add to that budget pressure and debt. Over the same period, central banks have become the key purchasers of booming government debt. That has massively expanded the money supply, which inevitably has to find a home, usually driving up the stock market or raising the price of other capital assets such as houses. Australia has now joined most other developed nations in using such policies, and in November 2020, Treasury Secretary Steven Kennedy noted that population ageing had been a key factor in this. We have come later to this than most, mainly because we have aged more slowly.

Inflation is also low. Stage-two monetary policies of 'fighting inflation first' have become an historical curiosity, with most central banks struggling to reach their inflation targets. Stage three is a brave new world indeed, and in stage four we will need to be braver still.

STAGE FOUR: THE BOOMERS DIE OUT

Hopefully I have conveyed the need for government to rethink the policies it used in the second stage of the population shock sufficiently to explain why I am not waiting until Australia reaches stage four to write this book. The fourth stage of the population shock will, after all, be the stage in which the overall size of the population begins to decline. It could be a little difficult for me to write about the demise of my own generation.

My former colleagues from the years I spent working in the Immigration Department regularly go for walks around Canberra together. We share stories of working for governments whose actions are now described as 'history' by my daughters and their contemporaries. We are aged in our sixties and seventies, but already there is talk of what's to come. Our conversations are bookended by news of who is sick, and who has died. One friend jokes that he now reads the obituary section of the newspaper first. This might sound depressing to younger people, but it is the way of life now for boomers—and also, the way of populations.

Before the COVID-19 pandemic, I was invited to Japan by the Australian National University and Tokyo University to talk about immigration policy. After decades of refusing to entertain immigration as a means of dealing with its demographic challenges, Japan is now realising its serious mistake. Unlike most of the developed world, which is still approaching stage four of the population shock, Japan has walked through the doorway and is firmly embedded there. The WAP ratio of all developed nations is now in decline, but Japan reached this landmark back in 1990. It has the oldest population on earth, already with a median age of over forty-seven—by comparison, Australia's median age remains well under forty. More than half of Japanese women are now past child-bearing age. Indeed, Japan's median age is barrelling towards fifty, a level never before reached by any major economy. Population decline is the inevitable next step after ageing, for all nations: for Japan, deaths already exceed births by 500 000 per annum, and by the end of this decade the gap may be a million per annum.

In stage four of the population shock, the annual number of births remains low and eventually drops even further as the portion of women over forty-five rises. For most developed nations, net migration is unlikely to be enough to stop the inevitable decline. Large numbers of the elderly boomer population will start to die out over the next 20–30 years, and in increasing numbers—the timing of this will vary from nation to nation. During this period, the rate of population ageing is likely to stabilise. That is, the baby boomer generation is so large that, as they die out, the WAP ratio will temporarily stabilise. Even the median age may, for a decade or so, stop rising.

However, once the baby boomer generation has passed away, the situation does not magically right itself from the 100-year population shock. The baby boomers were not only a very large generation but, as I have discussed, they included the first generation of women who could effectively control their own fertility. So long as couples continue to have an insufficient number of children to replace themselves—that is, substantially less than two births per woman, and in many cases well below 1.5 births per woman—population ageing will resume once the boomers have passed away.

Over the next decade or two, many more nations will move into the fourth stage. Population decline in Japan, Italy, Spain, Germany, South Korea, Taiwan, China, Russia, and most nations of Eastern Europe and Central Asia, will gradually accelerate. The annual number of deaths will rise strongly, and there's no evidence to suggest the number of births will grow in a meaningful way. A high median age combined with a low fertility rate and negligible immigration make population decline inevitable. It is just arithmetic.

China has the added problem of a very low proportion of women in its population, due to its now-discontinued one-child policy. The consequences for a country with a large excess of males are something the Chinese Government will have to manage. Heterosexual Chinese men will increasingly have to go overseas to find a partner, without whom they might never have children. The Chinese Government is already trying to attract back the young people in its diaspora, in part to alleviate this emerging problem. The result may be that China becomes a nation of net immigration, rather than one of net emigration, as it has been for the last forty years.

The 2020s and 2030s will be the first time in modern history that a number of the world's major economic powers, including the European Union, Japan, China and Russia, will simultaneously have significantly aged *and shrinking* populations.

Most of these nations have very little experience of managed migration. They will not be able to use immigration as readily as Australia can to manage a more gradual and controlled entry into stage four. The point in our future when deaths begin to exceed births will depend on our fertility rate and the level of net migration. If fertility remains or falls below the 1.66 births per woman recorded in 2019—the lowest in our history—and net migration is around zero, deaths will begin to exceed births within fifteen years and our population will start to shrink—and shrink increasingly rapidly. If we can keep our fertility rate from falling too much below the current rate, that will help delay the inevitable. If we can maintain a healthy level of net migration, that too will help make the adjustment less painful.

Ageing and decline will impact Australia's regional towns much earlier than our major cities because cities tend to attract young people looking for economic opportunities—this has been reversed during COVID-19 but that may be temporary. It will accelerate the demise of many small- and medium-sized country towns. The main exceptions will be towns like Forster-Tuncurry in New South Wales, Bongaree-Woorim in Queensland and Victor Harbour in South Australia, which have become retiree centres. The economies of these places are a bit different to the rest. They have the same low WAP ratios because most of the people who reside there live off superannuation, investment income and pensions. Those who do work earn comparatively low wages. This is due to low-wage employers such as retail, aged care, health care and—eventually—the funeral parlour being major employers in such towns. These retiree towns have a median age that will soon exceed sixty years old. But the difference is that they will, for a period, have a growing population as they attract more retirees from other parts of Australia.

Once a nation's population is severely aged and in ongoing decline, the prospect of a 'technical recession'—that is, two consecutive quarters of negative economic growth—will become more common, as has frequently been the case in Japan. As more nations move into the fourth stage of the population shock, economists will need a new definition for economic recession. The current definition was born out of the second stage and will be of limited use as developed nations move further into the third and fourth stages when negative economic growth becomes more common.

OUR POPULATION AND ECONOMIC OUTLOOK

When my two daughters were in primary school during the 1990s, there were a lot of arguments about the television. Ours was a big, heavy box of a thing, covered in laminate designed to look like wood. Its classy aesthetics aside, the most notable thing about our television was that there was only one of it. Oh, the bickering that went on. My eldest daughter was devoted to *Heartbreak High*, my youngest to cartoons on the ABC. My wife preferred a good BBC period drama, while I always campaigned valiantly for the cricket. After an argument over the screening of a World Cup qualifier versus *Melrose Place* threatened to divide the family forever, we relented. My wife and

I purchased a second television in a desperate move to restore harmony in the household.

The arrival of a second set led to some peculiar simultaneous screenings. On one occasion I recall the girls were watching Disney's original movie-length cartoon of *Alice in Wonderland* while I was watching reruns of a personal favourite, *Yes Minister*. For public servants of my generation, *Yes Minister* was both hilarious and the very best of training manuals. In this particular episode, Sir Humphrey Appleby, as the minister's head of the Department of Administrative Affairs, recounted the vast inconsistencies between the polar-opposite positions that governments can hold—often, he maintained, at the very same time. The governments he worked for had managed to be both pro-European and anti-European concurrently. Pausing to gather myself after fits of laughter, I glanced over at what my kids were watching. The evil Queen of Hearts had discovered someone had painted her roses red to keep her happy. Some people, fearful of their leaders, try their best to give them what they want, no matter how fanciful.

How Australia deals with immigration as we emerge from the COVID-19 pandemic will be crucial to determining the future of our population and our economy. Pursuing a slightly higher level of net migration would push back the inevitable day when deaths start to exceed the number of births. A lower level of net migration would bring that day forward. The 2021 *Intergenerational Report* has clearly signalled the government's intention to quickly ramp up net migration to around 235 000 per annum from 2024–25—the fastest rate of increase in net migration in our history. That also includes an assumed increase in the formal migration program from 160 000 per annum to 190 000 per annum from 2023–24. But the report provides no indication of how net migration of 235 000 per annum will be delivered. That is akin to sleepwalking into our future.

The increased level of migration is a reversal of Prime Minister Scott Morrison's March 2019 'population plan'. That plan included a reduction in the migration program 'ceiling' from 190 000 visas per annum to 160 000. The 'ceiling' concept was invented by then home affairs minister Peter Dutton to replace the longstanding approach of using an immigration 'target'. Neither the 'target' nor the 'ceiling' is contained in any legislation or regulation. They are purely administrative devices designed to give some indication of the overall number of permanent migration visas the government intends to grant each year. Dutton replaced the concept of a 'target' with a 'ceiling' of 190 000 places in 2017–18 to enable him to reduce the migration program to 168 000 without

Cabinet authority or any prior public announcement. In effect, Morrison's subsequent 'population plan' reducing the 'ceiling' to 160 000 per annum was really just an announcement of existing immigration policy as devised unilaterally by Dutton.

Somewhat bizarrely, Morrison's new 'population plan' made no actual mention of the government's planned future population for Australia. It was mostly another political announcement with little real substance other than some quite silly changes to existing regional migration visas designed to encourage more migrants to settle in regional Australia—visas which had actually declined in use from when Morrison had been immigration minister.

Morrison's new rationale for Dutton's earlier reduction of the migration program was to 'bust congestion'. It was a populist approach designed to win the approval of a voting public looking for someone to blame for their long commute, and to deflect attention away from the failure of successive governments to adequately plan infrastructure and services in our major cities. It's important to understand here that the migration program only reflects the number of permanent resident visas issued. This includes permanent residency being extended to people who are already in Australia, on student visas for example. By contrast, net migration represents the *actual* change in Australia's resident population from people movements. It includes Australian citizens returning home after living overseas or departing to live long term overseas, New Zealanders coming to stay or leave long term, international students, asylum seekers and others. Net migration is the number of people coming into Australia and staying for at least twelve months out of sixteen—for whatever reason—minus those going the other way. And when you're talking about congestion in Sydney or Melbourne, it doesn't matter if the bloke in the car next to you is a temporary entrant or a permanent one or a citizen. What matters is that he's also stuck in traffic and equally fed up with the situation. This makes net migration the more important measure when it comes to population fluctuations, economic impact and, indeed, congestion.

Within a month of announcing a congestion-busting cut to the migration program, the Morrison government's 2019 Budget forecast that Australia's population would grow at an unprecedented average of 450 000 per annum over the four-year forward estimates. This forecast relied on two key assumptions: first, that net migration would increase substantially, and second, that the fertility rate would do the same. At best, these assumptions can be described as heroic. They were actually a fraud perpetrated on the Australian public to support Frydenberg's boast about the budget forever being 'back in black'. The idea that we would grow the net number of people arriving to live here long term, while also pursuing the recently reduced 'ceiling' on the number of permanent visas issued, was an extraordinary leap of faith. The notion that Australian women would magically begin having more babies at a time when child care is inaccessible and prohibitively expensive, was a fallacy. There has only ever been one occasion when Australia's population has grown by more than 450 000 in a single calendar year, and that was back in 1971. How the government will 'bust congestion' with a population growing at that rate over four years remains a mystery.

Scott Morrison has very carefully curated his ordinary Aussie dad routine. To quote another ordinary Aussie dad, Darryl Kerrigan, they must have been dreaming. Despite obviously being pie-in-the-sky stuff, that population growth dream underpinned the 2019 Budget. The only reason that Budget was able to forecast real economic growth climbing to 3 per cent per year for ten years was because of the supporting projected population growth and the fantasy of productivity growth returning to 1.5 per cent per annum. The only reason it could forecast the creation of 250 000 jobs per year for five years was because of the projected increase in net migration. The only reason it could forecast its headline-grabbing series of surpluses for the following ten years was, again, because of the projected population growth. The 2019 Budget was a duplicitous election document that Treasury should never have signed off on. It will forever be a stain on the department's reputation.

We will never know how the Australian electorate might have voted in the election, held mere weeks later, had they been aware of the record population growth the government was projecting. Prime Minister Morrison spoke publicly, loudly and repeatedly about his decision to cut immigration and bust congestion during the election campaign. But he never mentioned the record levels of net migration and projected baby boom that his Budget relied on. In retrospect, the government may be able to explain away its valiant assumptions as a casualty of the COVID-19 recession. But that would be another falsehood. The population growth forecasts were a fantasy well before the pandemic. They were never going to eventuate. In 2019 itself, the forecast growth fell short by over 80 000 people.

COVID-19 has, of course, completely changed what Australia's future path might otherwise have been, including in terms of population levels and our economic and budgetary position. By 2023, Australia's population is likely to be at least 1.24 million less than was forecast in the 2019 Budget.

In the 2021 Budget and *Intergenerational Report*, the Australian Government has forecast a once-off sharp increase in real economic growth for 2021–22 of 4.25 per cent, and then 2.6 per cent growth for the balance of the next forty years. This is based on an assumption that the movement of people within Australia will return to normal during 2021–22—that is, very few lockdowns—and international borders will reopen from mid-2022. The 2021–22 forecast relies on a very significant 5.5 per cent boost in household consumption as well as record levels of fiscal and monetary stimulus. The boost in economic growth and private consumption may be plausible given how far economic growth fell during the COVID-19 recession of the previous financial year, coupled with the large amounts of cash banked by well-off Australians (including the withdrawal of large amounts of superannuation) during a year spent saving in the face of economic uncertainty. But what of the years beyond that?

Because of the effects of compounding over many decades, even very small differences in forecast long-term annual real economic growth have very large impacts in terms of Australia's standard of living and the sustainability of government budgets. In the past four releases of the *Intergenerational Report*, treasurers have forecast average real economic growth for the 2020s and beyond at significantly varying levels, and as a result very different outcomes for budget balances and government debt. For example:

- Peter Costello in 2002 forecast real economic growth averaging 2 per cent annually, and relatively slow population growth, including net migration of 90 000 annually leading to an ongoing increase in budget deficits to 5 per cent of GDP by 2042 and continuously rising government debt.
- Costello in 2007 forecast real economic growth averaging a slightly higher 2.3 per cent annually, and slightly faster population growth, including net migration of 110 000 annually leading to budget deficits rising to a smaller 3.75 per cent per annum by 2046–47 and net debt of 30 per cent of GDP.
- Wayne Swan in 2010 forecast real economic growth averaging 2.7 per cent annually, and even faster population growth, including net migration of 180 000 annually leading to budget surpluses until 2031–32 and then budget deficits rising to 2.75 per cent of GDP by 2049–50, and an even smaller net debt of 20.2 per cent of GDP by 2049–50.

- Joe Hockey in 2015 forecast real economic growth averaging 2.8 per cent annually, and population growth that was faster still, including net migration of 215 000 per annum—combined with big cuts to social welfare and health spending, he forecast sustained surpluses from 2019–20 and zero net debt by 2031–32.

Thus, very small tweaks to forecast annual real economic growth can dramatically change the long-term outlook. The ten-year plan that Josh Frydenberg outlined in his 'back in black' 2019 Budget was even more optimistic for the 2020s. It forecast real economic growth averaging 3 per cent annually, and warp-speed population growth, including net migration averaging 268 000 per annum. We don't need *Sesame Street*'s Count von Count to tell us that these numbers are much, much bigger than the ones that previously applied for exactly the same decade—although his cackle is indeed appropriate in these circumstances. The experience of all major developed economies, as well as Australia's, shows that once a country's WAP ratio has peaked, real economic growth, including per-capita growth, weakens. Here in Australia, our WAP ratio hit that peak in 2009, and as expected, growth has been slower than it was in the decades preceding the peak.

Given the global experience of population ageing, Treasury Secretary Steven Kennedy appears to have been successful in restraining Josh Frydenberg to a forecast of long-term real economic growth of 2.6 per cent per annum. But even that more modest forecast is based on some heroic assumptions about population growth, participation and productivity. It is likely to be a compromise between the reality that Treasury can see and the political demands of the Treasurer. A lower level of economic growth, as is likely to be Treasury's real assessment, would of course mean even larger budget deficits and debt into the future, and the need for more urgent action.

AUSTRALIA'S FUTURE:
A MORE REALISTIC ASSESSMENT

My son-in-law Jeremy is a lifelong Carlton supporter and an eternal optimist. Regardless of how dire the season has been, he can always visualise a premiership on the horizon—usually, the very distant horizon. For a supporter of a footy club that hasn't won a premiership since 1995, this is a truly impressive delusion. As the trading period begins ahead of each new season, he starts to get excited. He maintains that the club has been in an essential 'rebuilding phase' and that this will be their year. Carlton have a new list, worthy of excitement. They have new recruits who are champions in the making. They have a new coach who will change the way they play. While the present looks awfully grim, Jeremy has an uncanny ability to project forward a few years or more with unreasonable positivity.

In this, my son-in-law is not unlike an Australian treasurer. Treasurers are always wildly optimistic about how the economy will be performing under their far-sighted policies. Jeremy always insists that his team's current strategy will deliver amazing results. Similarly, treasurers also shape their reform agendas through an ideological prism, rather than designing their plans to meet the nature of the demographic, economic and environmental future we actually face. If Jeremy was honest with himself, he'd switch teams. But he's loyal to the Navy Blues. Just as Coalition governments are committed to budget austerity for health, education and welfare spending; wage suppression; the interests of big-business donors; and the bribing of voters with tax cuts that inevitably require more budget austerity and the denuding of public services. Just as Labor is loyal to the union movement, a tendency to rush the implementation of too many big ideas with big price tags, and lacklustre efforts to bring the community with them.

To forecast economic growth for the 2021 *Intergenerational Report*, Treasury has reverted to its 3Ps framework. By 3Ps, I mean the participation, productivity and population formulation for forecasting the future size of an economy which former Treasury secretary Ken Henry initiated in the context of the first *Intergenerational Report* in 2002. By multiplying the number of hours worked with the outputs created during those hours with the size of the population, we can calculate the GDP of a nation. It follows, therefore, that by multiplying the expected changes in each of these inputs, we can come up with a fair indication of the future rate of real economic growth.[14]

No set of forecasts is ever fail-safe. The world is full of too many variable events (exhibit A: a global pandemic) for that. There will also be fluctuations in the economic cycle that will at times give different impressions of the state of the economy. However, we can safely use the 3Ps framework to discuss the possible long-term average for participation, productivity and population change during the next few decades. And I have the luxury of being able to do so without the need to worry about an upcoming election. My aim is to give Australians a yardstick with which to judge estimates for the same variables the Treasurer has published in his 2021 *Intergenerational Report*.

This may help readers to form their own judgements about the 3Ps, forecast economic growth and projected budget balances the Treasurer has suggested.

Participation

Australia had a historically high labour-participation rate prior to COVID-19. It peaked in August 2019 with 66.2 per cent of adult Australians in the labour force. Remember that, at that time, adult Australians in the labour force included around two million relatively young temporary entrants, most of whom were counted as part of the resident population. Most would have had to work to survive, as they had no access to social security. Unsurprisingly, the number of working Australians then fell sharply during the initial period of the pandemic, as businesses were forced to close their doors: some temporarily, others forever. Participation dipped to 62.7 per cent in May 2020, increased to 66.3 per cent in March 2021, and is forecast in the 2021 *Intergenerational Report* to gradually fall to 63.6 per cent by 2060–61.

The Australian electorate has become accustomed to governments speaking about participation and unemployment as the be-all-and-end-all measures of economic virility, but the number of people employed can actually be quite misleading because it includes anyone who works at least an hour per week. Specifically, participation and unemployment rates do not distinguish between full-time, part-time, casual and gig economy work. Consider the twenty-something casual barista who needs the security and income of a permanent job but his employer won't offer it. Or the new mother who wants to return to work as a full-time accountant but can't find or afford child care and so is stuck on two days a week. Or the sixty-something guy who used to work in manufacturing but can't afford to retrain and so drives a few hours a week for Uber instead.

This is why 3Ps modelling uses hours worked, rather than the participation rate, as the basis for forecasting economic growth—unfortunately, 'hours worked' does not start with the letter 'p'. Despite higher participation rates, the number of hours worked per adult per week in Australia fell from thirty-five in 1978–79 to thirty-two in 2018–19.[15] There are now more and more households in which the adults have work, but not enough of it to be comfortable. Next time the government proudly announces a fall in the unemployment rate, remember that it could mask a more sombre reality for many families.

The decline in average hours worked per adult per week is partly being driven by the rising number of retirees. The total number of retirees in Australia increased from 2.9 million in 2008–09 to almost 3.9 million in 2018–19—these figures are net of deaths, as around 150 000 retirees currently die every year. The net additional number of retirees in the population will continue to rise throughout the 2020s, and at a faster rate as more baby boomers reach retirement age. This means the rate of growth in total hours worked that Australia achieved during the second stage of the population shock will be impossible to repeat during the 2020s and into the 2030s. Once we are past the one-off surge in hours worked after the domestic lockdowns and reopening of international borders, the government cannot reasonably forecast average growth in hours worked in the 2020s and 2030s at much higher than 1.5 per cent per annum— it's more likely to be lower as population ageing increases further.

Productivity

Labour productivity will be crucial in preventing the Australian economy, and our standard of living, from going backwards—that is, the quantity of output produced for each hour worked. Productivity is how efficiently an economy uses each unit of labour. The more productive an economy is, the greater the potential returns on the capital invested, and the greater the prospect of a wage rise—assuming government policy doesn't continue to actively keep wages down. The only way for a high-wage economy like ours to remain competitive is if each person's contribution continues to grow.

Growth in labour productivity declined markedly in Australia over the last decade, and it was just as bad for the rest of the developed world. This is consistent with the research on ageing and workforce productivity. Even with significant technological advancement, productivity growth slowed once the nations of the developed world collectively entered stage three of the population shock. Why? Because with comparatively fewer of us in the peak-productivity age group of 40–50 years old compared with the number of retirees, and with persistently weak private consumption expenditure leading to weak business investment, there was no other feasible result.

The past four releases of the *Intergenerational Report* have forecast a fall in Australia's productivity growth through the 2020s. In 2015, treasurer Joe Hockey said that our labour productivity would grow more slowly in the decade the world has just entered than was forecast by Peter Costello, averaging 1.5 per cent annually. But while our productivity growth generally has been higher than that of many developed nations over the past ten years, it has already gone well below Joe Hockey's forecast for the 2020s, averaging 0.8 per cent per annum in the period 2013–19.

The 2021 *Intergenerational Report* forecasts a return to the average productivity growth that Australia has experienced over the past thirty years. That's a growth rate of 1.5 per cent annually—the same as Hockey's forecast. Professor Janine Dixon, as reported in the *Australian Financial Review*, understandably argues this is overly optimistic.[16] It ignores population ageing and the experience of developed nations across the world. Indeed, it ignores our own experience of the last ten years. As we continue to age, with comparatively fewer Australians in the most-productive forty-something age bracket, average productivity growth will likely move further away from Hockey's 2015 and Frydenberg's 2021 prediction.

Treasury provides little plausible explanation for why it thinks productivity growth will return to stage two population shock standards once we are deep in the third stage. Without major economic reform to boost aggregate demand and thereby increase business investment, forecasting such growth makes no sense. It would be prudent for Australians to ask what economic reforms the Morrison government is planning in order to achieve this ambitious rate of productivity growth, other than its usual supply-side prescriptions or tax cuts for higher-income earners, which simply will not be appropriate for the third stage of the population shock. Certainly, the government's ideological dislike of Australia's public universities, as well as its refusal to take advantage of the biggest transformation in energy and transport technology in our lifetimes, are unlikely to be helpful.

For the 2020s and 2030s, the government cannot reasonably assume long-term average productivity growth much higher than the 0.8 per cent per annum achieved during the period 2013–19, especially given the experience around the developed world, where productivity growth has been lower still since developed nations collectively passed their WAP ratio peak. Without genuine reform, it may indeed turn out to be even lower.

Population

The Treasurer wants a return to higher levels of population growth, mainly through higher net migration, as quickly as possible. Other than genuine economic reform that will increase aggregate demand, something Frydenberg and Morrison have shown they are allergic to, this is one of the few other ways to deliver the 2.6 per cent per annum economic growth the government has forecast. Treasury Secretary

Kennedy said as much in November 2020, and the RBA has also been publicly supportive of returning to higher levels of net migration. State governments, including the current conservative NSW administration, are also urging an increase in skilled migration and overseas students. Universities are desperate for more international students to repair their financial positions post the pandemic and the loss of some 17 000 university jobs. And farmers want more temporary entrants to work for them, albeit for very little pay and appalling living conditions. As always, the business community, particularly the property sector, will be on the government's back to boost net migration—and fast.

The tourism and hospitality industry are excited about Immigration Minister Alex Hawke allowing overseas students to work as many hours as they wish in the sector, irrespective of whether classes are in session. This will lock-in a low-quality reputation for Australia's international education industry. And the Prime Minister has said we will have an agriculture visa for people from the Association of Southeast Asian Nations. The Morrison Government appears intent on making sure Australia becomes the low-skill guest worker society my former colleagues and I in the Department of Immigration thought Australia should never become.

In the 2021 Budget and *Intergenerational Report*, the Treasurer predicts that population growth for 2020–21 will be 32 000, and for 2021–22 it will be 42 000, as restrictions on international movements are assumed to remain in place until mid-2022. Frydenberg then forecasts this increasing to 218 000 in 2022–23, 328 000 in 2023–24 and 362 000 in 2024–25—around 1.37 per cent. While these projections are more plausible than the fanciful 450 000 per annum Treasury forecast in the 2019 Budget, they do require close scrutiny. A substantial part of the revision is that Treasury now expects annual births over the next few years to be flat, followed by a slight increase after that. The increase in births is partly linked to a projected increase in net migration: more young adults usually means more children. The key, thus, is the forecast for net migration.

NET MIGRATION

Through the late 1990s, while working at the Immigration Department, I had countless conversations with businessmen in flash suits and shiny shoes who would arrive at the department's offices in Canberra toting bulging briefcases and lots of bright ideas. The famous brutalist concrete architecture of those offices matched the tone of the visitors—impudent and in your face. They would relax into the armchairs in my office and unload their wisdom: 'We should massively increase our migration program. More migrants will grow the economy! They'll create jobs and help more businesses succeed. And if we aren't getting enough visa applications that meet the criteria, then we should simply change the criteria. Drop our standards a bit. Easy!' What these enthusiastic individuals failed to understand was that the criteria existed for a reason. These had been carefully crafted to deliver Australia the many benefits of migration, while also supporting the employment of Australians and protecting migrant workers from exploitation. 'Doesn't matter,' the business types would insist, grinning. 'Just turn up the numbers, fiddle the dial. That way we'll sell more stuff and be able to hire more people!'

In addition to the fertility rate, the level of net migration will determine the rate at which Australia's population ages and the point at which deaths begin to exceed births. A higher rate of net migration results in a slower rate of ageing, and the point at which deaths exceed births is pushed into the future, possibly well into the second half of this century. A very low level of net migration results in an accelerated rate of ageing, and in deaths exceeding births possibly within the next 20–30 years. That likely explains Treasury's desire to increase net migration quickly, and to a comparatively high level. If achieved, the forecast increase in net migration would represent by far the steepest increase in our history.

A commonly held community assumption is that governments can increase or reduce net migration with the flick of a switch. The belief that setting and delivering the desired level of net migration is as simple as choosing chocolate rather than vanilla ice cream is wildly misguided. Nothing could be further from the truth. While the Abbott government tried to lock in high migration through the largest permanent migration program in our history, the rapid deterioration of the labour market under Tony Abbott's leadership ultimately gave us the lowest level of net migration in a decade. Australian and NZ citizens, as well as some categories of migrants and temporary residents, left this country in larger numbers, searching for better opportunities elsewhere.

After the 1991 recession, it took a decade for net migration to recover to late-1980s levels. Yet Treasury projects that within three years of the COVID-19 recession, net migration will rapidly increase to 235 000 per annum and remain at that level for the next forty years. This forecast is apparently based on an average of net migration in the years prior to COVID. That is a period when Abbott boosted permanent migration but delivered low net migration because of a weak economy. And Turnbull and Morrison cut permanent migration to 'bust congestion'; allowed a boom in trafficked and mostly unsuccessful asylum seekers who are still in Australia, largely working on farms; choked off employer-sponsored and skilled independent visas; unlawfully limited the number of partner visas; promoted a massive increase in overseas students, before tightening student visas from India and Nepal; and entered into an ongoing diplomatic fight with China, our major source of overseas students. Remember, students have in recent years made up over 40 per cent of net migration—immigration levels go largely where student visa policy goes.

Which of these policies does Treasury expect will continue or change for the next forty years? The 2021 *Intergenerational Report* provides surprisingly little detail on how the forecast level of net migration will be delivered. Indeed, in May 2021, the head of the Department of Home Affairs, Mike Pezzullo, said he was not even aware of the forecast that his department will primarily be responsible for delivering. This is just a recipe for badly managed immigration. It is essential the government develop a realistic plan for how it will deliver its forecast level of net migration, and communicate this widely to assist planning by all Commonwealth/state government agencies and industries.

For the forecast net migration of 235 000 per annum to be realised, a whole bunch of things must happen. There must be a rapid return to a strong economy, and a much lower level of unemployment with strong growth in hours worked. There will also need to be a significant positive shift in the net movement of Australian and NZ citizens compared with the situation pre-COVID, and steady growth in the stock of temporary entrants, particularly students, temporary graduates, provisional visa holders and possibly even asylum seekers.

Over the decade prior to COVID-19, net migration averaged 215 000 annually. For 2019, actual net migration was 247 620, compared with the 2019 Budget forecast of 271 000, but it included an unprecedented 100 280 people on visitor visas who did not leave. More importantly, net migration was trending downward well before COVID-19. This was due to a combination of factors, including government changes to immigration policy and a weakening economy. Once internal and international movement fully resume—*if* they fully resume—there are three broad possible outcomes for net migration to Australia in the second half of the 2020s: either Australia falls well short of Treasury's forecast increase; or the government increases the permanent intake to 190 000 per annum, and makes other changes to immigration policy settings to try and deliver Treasury's net migration forecast; or the government takes significant risks in rapidly growing the number of overseas students, temporary graduates and farm labourers to deliver its forecast, but maintains the permanent intake at 160 000 per annum.

The 2021 *Intergenerational Report* assumes the permanent migration program will return to 190 000 per annum from 2023–24, while leaving the humanitarian program at the reduced level of 13 750. No formal announcement of this has yet been made. Given the Prime Minister's cynical message about cutting immigration to bust congestion ahead of the 2019 election, the absence of an official announcement is not surprising. Any such declaration of an increase will likely be left until after the next election. The bulk of any larger migration program from 2023–24 would have to be delivered through the general points-tested category, where the migrant has no employer sponsor. With the wait for social security extended to four years after arrival, these new migrants would desperately need employment to survive, possibly in a weak labour market. The risk of worker exploitation in these circumstances is severe.

Achieving average long-term net migration of 235 000 per annum without increasing the permanent migration program, would necessitate the government taking major risks with temporary entry policy, such as the recent announcement to give full-time work rights to overseas students to work in the tourism and hospitality industry. This is likely to make Australia attractive to students more interested in a work visa than study, and will increase the risk of more temporary entrants being unable or unwilling to leave, but unable to secure permanent residence. Furthermore, for the net migration target to be met, the number of temporary residents in Australia would need to approach 2.5 million by the end of 2030—there are currently around 1.7 million temporary residents living here, despite having been told by the Prime Minister to go home early in the pandemic. Most temporary residents, including the asylum seekers who initially came to Australia on visitor visas, don't have access to government welfare support. In a weak labour market, the risk of them being exploited, of being subjected to wage theft and abuse, grows. It is possible that many would become destitute and reliant on charity. There are already large numbers of temporary residents in Australia who are living in such conditions, and it is an area of policy that requires attention beyond the government's current tokenism. The spate of food-delivery cyclist deaths on the roads of Australia's major cities in recent times is an indication of the pressure that temporary residents, such as overseas students, are under.

Over the past five to six years, Australia has experienced its fifth and by far its largest wave of asylum seekers. Prior to COVID-19, asylum seekers were contributing around 25 000 people per annum to net migration (around 12 per cent). This latest wave is unlike any that have come before. Approval rates for asylum seekers in the previous four waves were generally well over 90 per cent; those for asylum seekers in the fifth wave are generally below 5 per cent. The latest wave has all the characteristics of a labour-trafficking scam, particularly to undertake farm labour. Yet a government allegedly strong on border control is happy to sweep the issue under the carpet.

An ABC investigation of foreign-language newspapers by journalist Isobel Roe found that of 3000 job advertisements, around 90 per cent were advertising on the basis of below-minimum wages.[17] This further highlights the endemic nature of the problem. Other indicators of the magnitude of the problem include the fact that, to date, twenty-two people on the relatively small Pacific island Seasonal Worker Program visa have died; the reluctance of farmers to sign up to the 'fair farms' initiative; and a report by The McKell Institute that backpackers picking fruit are being paid as little as $3 per hour and being forced to pay exorbitant rents for limited accommodation.[18]

The underpayment of temporary migrants was a focus of the 2019 Migrant Workers' Taskforce, which noted in its final report that this 'is a significant problem that has adverse effects on individuals, law-abiding employers and the community in general'.[19] In its response to the final report, the government claimed that it had 'already taken unprecedented steps to protect all vulnerable workers, including migrant workers'.[20] If the government thinks it has done enough to address the problem, it has its head in the sand.

While the government agreed 'in principle' to all the recommendations of the taskforce, the magnitude of the problem is well beyond the capacity of the Fair Work Ombudsman, even if it were given more money, much stronger powers, and if much greater penalties were instituted for employers and labour-hire companies who exploit migrant workers. In 2019–20, the FWO received 19 345 reports of suspected employer breaches, an increase of 17 per cent over the previous year. Yet it was only able to litigate cases of underpayment on behalf of some twenty-five people. It would be impossible for the FWO to properly follow up even a small portion of the reports of underpayment and exploitation it receives, particularly those that take place on farms well away from the major cities. Moreover, the number of reports of exploitation are likely just the tip of the iceberg, as many temporary entrants and unsuccessful asylum seekers are too afraid to report breaches or would lack confidence in any real action being taken—the FWO's actions against 7-Eleven since 2008 notwithstanding.

Without strengthening the role of unions in this space, and without much stronger laws against wage theft than the current weak measures that have been proposed (and now withdrawn), cases of exploitation of temporary entrants will continue to rise. At the same time, however, the government is under intense pressure from universities, private Vocational Education and Training colleges and state governments to loosen the tighter student visa criteria introduced in September 2019; that is, to allow the entry of more students whose financial capacity has not been properly checked. In a weak labour market, this is extremely dangerous for students who are a long way from family and their usual support networks. And there's pressure from the tourism industry to boost the number of working holiday-makers. How the Morrison government balances these competing pressures will be a major challenge if it is to deliver the net migration forecast of 235 000 per annum.

An alternative option is for the government to leave migration arrangements largely as they were immediately prior to COVID-19. This would mean that long-term average net migration during the 2020s would be closer to 175 000 per annum than the forecast 235 000. A slower build-up of long-term temporary entrants living in Australia would mean fewer challenges for those who cannot find a pathway to permanent residence due to a weak labour market, but who do not wish to return home, and it would limit growth in the exploitation of temporary entrants. Assuming a natural increase of around 125 000 per annum, Australia's total population would grow by 300 000 per annum in the 2020s—that's more than 50 000 per year less than the 2021 *Intergenerational Report* projections and 150 000 less than Treasury's projections in the 2019 Budget.

With weak growth in monthly hours worked per adult, as well as weak productivity growth, that level of population growth would make the 2021 *Intergenerational Report* forecast of real economic growth of 2.6 per cent per annum an impossibility—especially if the Morrison government remains reluctant to recognise that Australia is now firmly in stage three of the 100-year population shock.

Without genuine economic reform that boosts aggregate demand, average real economic growth over the 2020s is likely to be closer to Peter Costello's original forecast of 2 per cent per annum. That would still be well above average real economic growth in comparable economies once they have been in stage three of the population shock. This includes 1.31 per cent per annum in the EU, 0.91 per cent in Japan, 1.61 per cent in Canada, 1.14 per cent in the United Kingdom and 1.76 per cent in the United States. All of the above economic growth rates were calculated before the COVID-19–induced recession.

But a significantly lower level of real economic growth than forecast in the 2021 *Intergenerational Report* would have serious consequences for the sustainability of current budget settings.

WHAT'S MISSING FROM THE 2021 *INTERGENERATIONAL REPORT*?

In addition to geopolitical tensions, climate change and the threat of more pandemics, the major challenge of the twenty-first century will be population ageing and decline, and the consequences of that for greater wealth and income inequality.

The coming decades present an enormous threat to the prosperity Australia has achieved over the past seventy years. During the 2020s and 2030s, all developed nations will move deeper into the third stage of the population shock. Many will enter the fourth stage as their populations start shrinking, including in Japan, Russia, continental Europe, Central Asia, South Korea, Taiwan and China. Notably, China will be among those nations that enter the fourth stage at some point in the 2020s. China has been the world's engine room of economic growth for the last twenty years and is Australia's major trading partner. Its population decline will inevitably impact its economic growth and consequently our economy, which will itself be moving steadily deeper into stage three.

During the second stage of the population shock, the key economic challenge was surging growth in private consumption expenditure and inadequate capacity to keep up with that growth in demand, hence the need for policies such as 'keeping a lid on inflation'. The key challenge in the third and fourth stages will be persistently weak and eventually declining private consumption expenditure and excess productive capacity in many businesses. This will be exacerbated by the declining wage share of GDP. Weak private consumption expenditure across the developed world will make businesses increasingly reluctant to invest in boosting productive capacity. This will be made worse by the Morrison government's reluctance to be part of the current environmentally led technology revolution in both energy and transport.

Developed nations like Australia will need to make major adjustments to cope with population ageing and rising inequality in ways that are anathema to their past thinking on economic and budget management. While Australia's population will continue to grow for longer than most developed nations, aggregate demand will remain persistently weak. As a result, policy responses such as cutting company taxes, maintaining excessive tax concessions for capital income, cutting taxes for higher-income earners, and industrial relations reforms that make it easier to hire and fire, put downward pressure on wages and denigrate unions, simply will not work. Stimulatory monetary policies, while unavoidable, will also be largely ineffective and perhaps even counterproductive, as they could exacerbate existing wealth inequality and increase household debt.

If we accept Thomas Piketty's finding in *Capital in the Twenty-First Century* that inequality increases if economic growth is less than the return on capital, then it is almost inevitable that, as populations age, inequality will continue to grow—perhaps even grow faster. Put another way, the wages and wealth of average workers tend to rise in line with the rate of economic growth, while the income and wealth of the owners of capital tend to rise with the rate of return on capital. In Australia, one example of the rate of return on capital is the average rate of return of super-annuation funds over the last ten years: 7.6 per cent per annum, compared with economic growth of 2–3 per cent. The large differential between economic growth and the return on capital will further increase inequality and put downward pressure on aggregate demand. In turn, that will further slow economic growth. And so on.

While the Morrison government may continue to argue that inequality has not increased very much in recent times, and that their policies do not contribute to this, that is very much about playing with statistics to try and disguise what we all can see. The extent to which wealth inequality has increased is heavily understated, as official statistics often cannot capture the full extent of the wealth of the very rich due to the use of offshore tax havens, family trusts and creative accounting. In the United Kingdom, for example, the Resolution Foundation suggests that around £800 billion in wealth of the richest 1 per cent of UK citizens is being missed by official statistics.[21] In Australia, the Morrison government often uses taxable income rather than actual income as a way of disguising the extent to which inequality has increased. Of course, if we accept that taxable income is a true measure of a person's income, then Donald Trump would be categorised as a very poor man in the official statistics. In Australia, we also have a peculiar exemption that excuses 1119 proprietary companies from having to publish their accounts—companies mainly owned by private individuals who are among Australia's most wealthy. All such factors disguise the true extent of income and wealth inequality in official statistics.

It is against this background that Piketty argues strongly for an inheritance tax targeted at the very wealthy as a means of helping to meet the costs of an ageing population. Among developed nations, Australia is unusual in not having an inheritance tax. While the Organisation for Economic Co-operation and Development average is an inheritance tax of 15 per cent, in Australia, the very idea of an inheritance tax on the very wealthy has become politically toxic, driven by campaigns run by some of Australia's leading billionaires, keen to protect their wealth. The impact of the COVID-19 recession in further boosting the wealth of the top 0.1 per cent of the population may force a rethink in some developed nations.[22] Scott Morrison has argued that this is the politics of 'envy', even though many of the uber-wealthy have acquired their wealth through government tax and regulatory concessions granted by successive governments.

For the past fifty years, Australian governments have generally sought to grow the economic pie by supporting businesses to invest and expand in response to a growing population and strongly rising private consumption. The idea was that the benefits would eventually trickle down to ordinary Australians. Governments have consistently assumed that 'growing the economic pie' was preferable to 'better distributing the economic pie', and that the two were mutually exclusive. They are not. In an era of persistently weak private consumption expenditure associated with Australia's ageing population, better distributing our economic pie becomes more important than ever as the best means of supporting private consumption and thereby growing that pie. In a 1937 lecture titled 'Some Economic Consequences of a Declining Population', John Maynard Keynes pointed out that 'with a stationary population we shall … be absolutely dependent for the maintenance of prosperity and civil peace on policies of increasing consumption by a more equal distribution of incomes'.[23]

Policies aimed at reducing income and wealth inequality may be the only way to prevent private consumption expenditure from remaining weak, and hence the Australian economy from stagnating and eventually shrinking. Our governments will need to aggressively pursue policies that boost the wages share of GDP rather than just forecasting this and then pursuing policies that do the opposite. This is not about the so-called 'politics of envy'. It's about levelling the playing field rather than continuing with policies designed to give a 'free kick' to owners of capital and to the usual rent-seekers who seem to be able to lobby for the regulations that benefit them. Fairness is not about green-eyed jealousy. Fairness is the way most people in a society want to live. And no society can survive if the wages share of the economy continuously falls, as it has been doing in Australia since the 1970s.

The Morrison government set politics and ideology aside during its early response to the COVID-19 pandemic. However, while the 2021 *Intergenerational Report* has acknowledged our ageing population will continue to result in ongoing budget deficits, it failed to outline a plan to address the economic consequences of ageing. The policy prescriptions of Keynes, Joseph Stiglitz, Krugman and Piketty to reduce income and wealth inequality to boost private consumption appear to be a bridge too far. In a developed world that is in stage three of the population shock and increasingly moving into stage four, those policy prescriptions appear the only way that we can effectively support private consumption and thereby enable more businesses to survive. Business groups and leaders also need to reconsider their long-term approach to wages, if for no other reason than their own self-interest. If wages continue to stall, in a shrinking developed world there will be insufficient demand for the very goods and services those businesses are seeking to sell. After all, the people whose wages they have so effectively minimised are also their customers.

Some will argue that allowing higher wages as repeatedly suggested by the RBA would increase unemployment. The general unemployment rate will undoubtedly continue to fluctuate with the economic cycle. However, the number of people in long-term unemployment, which has been steadily rising for a decade, should seriously worry governments. The assumed link between the long-term unemployed and wages growth appears to have been broken.

In a 2012 speech, Gina Rinehart, Australia's richest woman and the inheritor of vast wealth, said, 'Africans want to work, and its workers are willing to work for less than $2 per day. Such statistics make me worry for this country's future'.[24] Rinehart was of course more worried about her own wealth and the ability of her companies to exploit their workers than for Australia's future. While many in the Morrison government will say they disagree with Rinehart's comments, forcing down wages is part of the DNA of conservative governments, as demonstrated by the

Howard government's WorkChoices legislation and the more recent industrial relations 'reforms' which have been temporarily postponed.

Ironically, the Business Council of Australia recently released a report expressing concern with the slow rate of wages growth in Australia.[25] Yet it is BCA members and members of similar employer bodies who fight tooth and nail against any wage rise the workers in their companies might ask for. These employer bodies also enlist the help of governments to enact 'industrial relations reforms' such as WorkChoices, as well as measures to limit any increase in minimum wages and maximise casualisation of the workforce, and they decry any increase in public sector wages as a waste of money. It is of course largely BCA members who have driven down the number of people covered by enterprise bargaining agreements, a key means by which workers access increased wages. (The BCA also continues to argue for a self-serving cut to the company tax rate for large companies, despite the state of government finances, the inexorable boom in the stock market and the huge tax concessions on capital income.)

Josh Frydenberg needs to break from the traditional thinking that 'keeping a lid on wage growth' is part of the treasurer's job description. Forecasting strong wage growth into the future without adopting policies to facilitate that growth is nothing more than a lie. We cannot build an Australia with rising living standards unless business, Treasury and the RBA are able to reconcile their contradictory views on unions. Weak unions mean wage theft and exploitation continue to run rampant, especially as the government has now decided to follow the lead of the United States and many European nations in allowing Australia to become a low-skill guest worker society.

Given the political ideology in this space over the last fifty years, allowing for more powerful unions feels next to impossible. But, once again, the pandemic proved that Morrison and his government were willing to compromise on ideology in a time of crisis. We can only hope that openly negotiating in good faith with unions on industrial relations won't be a bridge too far for Scott Morrison. He could take a leaf out of Bob Hawke's book on how to build a better economy and society.

Another challenge for Morrison is the issue of government debt and deficit. Government debt as a portion of GDP has been rising across the developed world throughout the last decade. Even prior to the COVID-19 recession, debt was at levels not seen since World War II. Now, the situation is more acute. The Morrison government will want to reduce the deficit and begin repaying government debt. But against the background of an ageing population, including in Australia's major trading partners, that will be much more difficult than in the past. Government budgets will certainly need to be well managed, but reducing services and support for Australians struggling to survive is not the way to do that in a time of weak aggregate demand and rising inequality. Ending the age of entitlement, as Joe Hockey called it, while ignoring the ongoing entitlements for the wealthy, will only further weaken aggregate demand and exacerbate the problems of ageing.

Population ageing will reduce growth in government revenue per capita. It will also limit wages growth and bracket creep. The eagerness of governments to offer tax cuts as a means of getting re-elected will need to be tempered, particularly tax cuts that favour the wealthy. The government's planned stage three tax cuts do exactly that and will cost $132 billion over five years. They must be urgently reconsidered. Governments need to prioritise the health, aged care and pension costs of an ageing population, which will be significant. The Royal Commission into Aged Care has recommended higher levels of spending to keep people safe, healthy and well cared for. This will be in addition to the large increase in spending needed to facilitate a growing aged-care population during the 2020s. The waiting list for older Australians seeking access to aged-care packages is already around 100 000, with waiting times often in excess of two years. The Morrison government's response to the royal commission has been half-hearted and completely lacking in the structural reforms to aged care that are needed.

To try and address the challenges of an ageing population, Frydenberg has highlighted increased superannuation balances to reduce a reliance on the age pension. Yet his government has pursued policies that have encouraged less-well-off Australians to withdraw their superannuation early, and considered the option of allowing them to raid their super balances to buy a house, as well as possibly postponing future increases in the superannuation guarantee. Most of the increase in superannuation balances the Treasurer has referred to would thus be among wealthy Australians who can more readily afford to take advantage of concessional contributions to super and lower super tax rates. They would not generally be eligible for the age pension in any case.

Over the last ten years, superannuation returns have averaged 7.6 per cent per annum, according to the government's MySuper website—well in excess of inflation, wage increases and economic growth. Combined with concessional tax arrangements, superannuation is increasingly becoming an estate planning tool for the rich rather than a means of enabling those less well-off to have a comfortable retirement and reduce the reliance on the age pension. In its own cautious way, the 2020 Retirement Income Review said as much. The cost to the Budget of these superannuation tax concessions for the wealthy will rise significantly over the next ten years. If Frydenberg is genuinely interested in addressing government debt and deficits, he would be well advised to revisit super-annuation policies that support the wealthy.

It may sound like I am living in a fantasy world, proposing that a conservative government consider such a suite of egalitarian policies. But eventually, the current government—or one of the governments that follows them—will have no choice. That Australia and the world are ageing is undeniable. That the economic crunch of stage four of the population shock will come is unavoidable. We can, however, take considered and deliberate steps to lessen the impact of ageing and soften the blow of eventual population decline.

That Australians deserve an honest framework and a workable plan for their long-term future is clear. The question remains whether the government is up to the task.

ACKNOWLEDGEMENTS

This book would not have been possible without the support of my wife Helen and my daughters Jamila and Miriam. The storytelling in this book reflects Jamila's extraordinary skills with the English language.

NOTES

1   Peter McDonald and Rebecca Kippen, 'Population Futures for Australia: the Policy Alternatives', Parliament of Australia, research paper 5, 12 October 1999.

2   Glenn Withers, 'A Younger Australia?', ANU Public Policy Discussion Paper, no. 63, March 1999, https://openresearch-repository.anu.edu.au/bitstream/1885/41930/1/dp_63.html (viewed July 2021).

3   Paul Ehrlich and Anne Ehrlich, *The Population Bomb*, Sierra Club–Ballantine, San Francisco, 1970.

4   Thomas Piketty, *Capital in the Twenty-First Century*, Belknap Press, Cambridge, MA, 2014.

5   Gianni La Cava, 'The Labour and Capital Shares of Income in Australia', *RBA Bulletin*, 21 March 2019.

6   Ibid.

7   Milton Friedman, 'A Friedman Doctrine: The Social Responsibility of Business Is to Increase Its Profits', *The New York Times*, 13 September 1970.

8   Charles Goodhart and Manoj Pradhan, *The Great Demographic Reversal: Ageing Societies, Waning Inequality, and an Inflation Revival*, Palgrave Macmillan, London, 2020.

9   Alvin H Hansen, 'Economic Progress and Declining Population Growth', *The American Economic Review*, vol. 29, no. 1, 1939, pp. 1–15.

10 Gunnar Myrdal, 'Population Problems and Policies', *The Annals of the American Academy of Political and Social Science*, vol. 197, no. 1, 1938, pp. 200–15.

11 Paul Krugman, 'Secular Stagnation, Coalmines, Bubbles, and Larry Summers', *The New York Times*, 16 November 2013.

12 Larry Summers, speech to the IMF Economic Forum, 8 November 2013, transcript at https://www.facebook.com/notes/randy-fellmy/transcript-of-larry-summers-speech-at-the-imf-economic-forum-nov-8-2013/585630634864563 (viewed July 2021).

13 United Nations, Department of Economic and Social Affairs, Population Division, *International Migration Report 2015*, 2016, https://www.un.org/en/development/desa/population/migration/publications/migrationreport/docs/MigrationReport2015.pdf (viewed July 2021).

14 It should be noted that the 3Ps framework is very much focused on the supply side of the economy. It assumes an adequate level of aggregate demand to generate adequate levels of productivity growth and hours worked. This is a very significant assumption indeed, given an ageing population in Australia and our major trading partners, rising inequality, and record levels of household debt.

15 Josh Frydenberg, *2021 Intergenerational Report: Australia over the Next 40 Years*, Commonwealth of Australia, June 2021, https://treasury.gov.au/sites/default/files/2021-06/p2021-182464.pdf (viewed July 2021).

16 Ronald Mizen, 'Budget Overshoots with "Optimistic" Productivity Gains', *Australian Financial Review*, 9 June 2021, https://www.afr.com/politics/federal/budget-overshoots-with-optimistic-productivity-gains-20210608-p57z78 (viewed July 2021).

17 Isobel Roe, 'Job Ads Targeting Migrants Overwhelmingly Offering Below the Minimum Wage', ABC News, 14 December 2020.

18 Edward Cavanough and Connor Wherrett, *Blue Harvest*, The McKell Institute, November 2020, https://mckellinstitute. org.au/app/uploads/McKell-Institute-Blue-Harvest-Final.pdf (viewed July 2021).

19 Australian Government, *Report of the Migrant Workers' Taskforce*, March 2019, https://www.ag.gov.au/industrial-relations/industrial-relations-publications/Documents/mwt_final_report.pdf (viewed July 2021).

20 Australian Government, 'Australian Government Response: Report of the Migrant Workers' Taskforce', March 2019.

21 Resolution Foundation, 'Top 1 Per Cent Has Almost £800 Billion More Wealth than Official Statistics Show', 3 January 2021, https://www.resolutionfoundation.org/press-releases/top-1-per-cent-has-almost-800-billion-more-wealth-than-official-statistics-show (viewed July 2021).

22 Davide Furceri, Prakash Loungani and Jonathan Ostry, 'How Pandemics Leave the Poor Even Farther Behind', IMFBlog, 11 May 2020.

23 John Maynard Keynes, 'Some Economic Consequences of a Declining Population', *Eugenics Review*, vol. 29, no. 1, 1937, https://www.ncbi.nlm.nih.gov/pmc/articles/PMC2985686/pdf/eugenrev00278-0023.pdf (viewed July 2021).

24 Peter Ryan, 'Aussies Must Compete with $2 a Day Workers: Rinehart', ABC News, 5 September 2012.

25 Business Council of Australia, 'Living on Borrowed Time', June 2021, https://www.bca.com.au/living_on_borrowed_time (viewed July 2021).